W9-CDX-535

KILLER ANIMALS
KOMODO DRAGONS
ON THE HUNT

by Janet Riehecky

Consultant:
Barbara J. Fox
Reading Specialist
North Carolina State University

Content Consultants:
Joe Maierhauser, President/CEO
Terry Phillip, Curator of Reptiles
Reptile Gardens
Rapid City, South Dakota

Capstone
press®

Mankato, Minnesota

Blazers is published by Capstone Press,
151 Good Counsel Drive, P.O. Box 669, Mankato, Minnesota 56002.
www.capstonepress.com

Copyright © 2009 by Capstone Press, a Capstone Publishers company. All rights reserved.
No part of this publication may be reproduced in whole or in part,
or stored in a retrieval system, or transmitted in any form or by any means,
electronic, mechanical, photocopying, recording, or otherwise,
without written permission of the publisher.
For information regarding permission, write to Capstone Press,
151 Good Counsel Drive, P.O. Box 669, Dept. R, Mankato, Minnesota 56002.
Printed in the United States of America

Library of Congress Cataloging-in-Publication Data
Riehecky, Janet, 1953–
    Komodo dragons: on the hunt/by Janet Riehecky.
    p. cm. — (Blazers. Killer animals)
    Includes bibliographical references and index.
    Summary: "Describes Komodo dragons, their physical features, how they hunt and kill, and
their role in the ecosystem" — Provided by publisher.
    ISBN-13: 978-1-4296-2318-6 (hardcover)
    ISBN-10: 1-4296-2318-7 (hardcover)
    1. Komodo dragon — Juvenile literature. I. Title.
QL666.L29R54 2009
597.95'968 — dc22   2008029832

Editorial Credits
Abby Czeskleba, editor; Kyle Grenz, designer; Wanda Winch, photo researcher

Photo Credits
Ardea/Valerie Taylor, 18–19
Getty Images Inc./Minden Pictures/JH Editorial/Cyril Ruoso, 14–15, 24–25; National
    Geographic/Joel Sartore, 26–27; Photographer's Choice/Michael Dunning, 10–11
Index Stock-photolibrary/Pacific Stock/James Watt, 28–29
Minden Pictures/Tui De Roy, 12
Peter Arnold/Biosphoto/Alain Compost, 16–17; Cyril Ruoso, 4–5, 8–9; Wolfgang Poelzer, 22–23
SeaPics/Marc Chamberlain, cover
Visuals Unlimited/Reinhard Dirscherl, 20–21
© WOLFGANG KAEHLER 2007/www.wkaehlerphoto.com, 6–7

1 2 3 4 5 6 14 13 12 11 10 09

TABLE OF CONTENTS

A Komodo dragon walks through the grass. Its yellow, forked tongue darts in and out of its mouth. A deer wanders nearby.

The Komodo dragon springs toward the deer. It bites the deer's leg. The deer falls to the ground. The dragon rips off large pieces of meat and swallows them whole. A second dragon joins the feast.

7

KILLER REPTILES

The Komodo dragon is a fierce **reptile**. It is the world's largest living lizard. Most Komodo dragons weigh more than 150 pounds (68 kilograms). They can grow to be more than 8 feet (2.4 meters) long.

reptile – a scaly-skinned animal that has the same body temperature as its surroundings

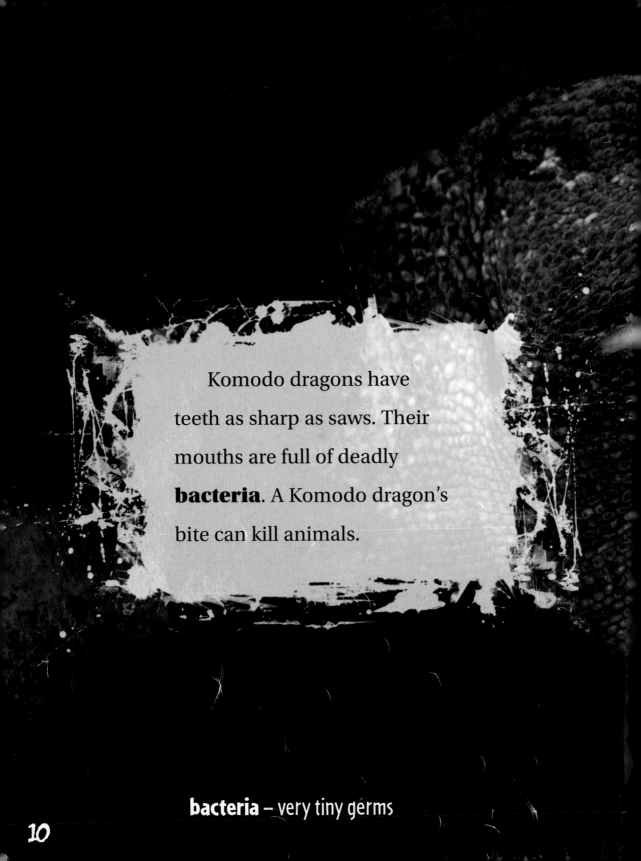

Komodo dragons have teeth as sharp as saws. Their mouths are full of deadly **bacteria**. A Komodo dragon's bite can kill animals.

bacteria – very tiny germs

KILLER FACT

A Komodo dragon has more than 50 kinds of bacteria in its mouth.

Komodo dragons also attack **prey** with their sharp claws. Their claws tear through skin and muscle.

prey – an animal hunted by another animal

Komodo dragons use their strong sense of smell while hunting. The **Jacobson's organ** helps them find food. The tongue picks up scents and carries them to the Jacobson's organ.

Jacobson's organ – an organ on the roof of a reptile's mouth

KILLER FACT

Komodo dragons can smell dead animals
from 2.5 miles (4 kilometers) away.

MAKING THE KILL

A Komodo dragon hides and waits for prey. It leaps out when a deer or wild pig runs by.

KILLER FACT

A Komodo dragon can run more than 10 miles (16 kilometers) per hour.

KILLER FACT

A Komodo dragon will follow a wounded animal for miles. The dragon eats the animal once it dies.

The dragon bites the animal's legs.
If the animal falls down, the dragon uses
its teeth and claws to kill the prey.

A Komodo dragon eats quickly. Its mouth stretches wide open. The dragon swallows huge pieces of meat.

Komodo Dragon Diagram

strong leg

long tail

scaly skin

sharp claw

HEADED FOR EXTINCTION?

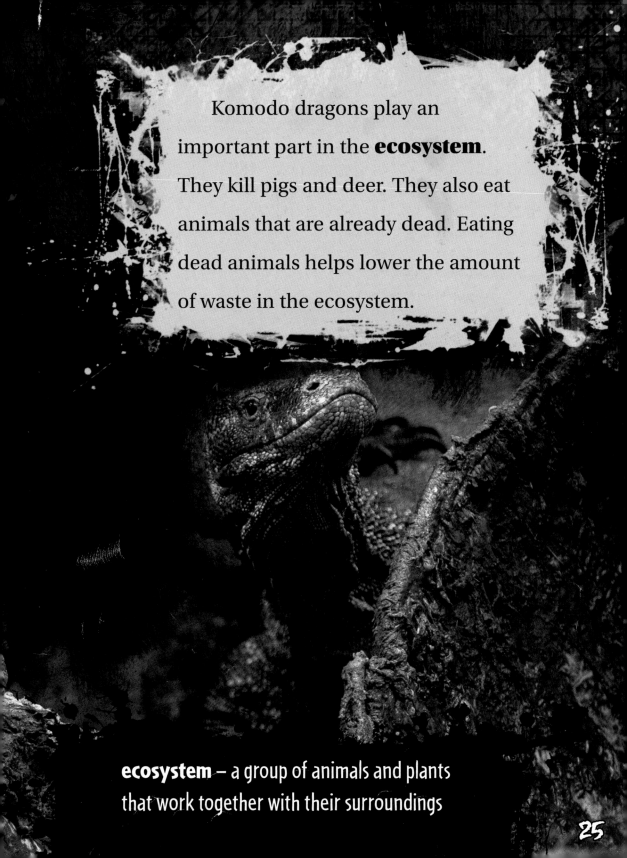

Komodo dragons play an important part in the **ecosystem**. They kill pigs and deer. They also eat animals that are already dead. Eating dead animals helps lower the amount of waste in the ecosystem.

ecosystem – a group of animals and plants that work together with their surroundings

KILLER FACT

Scientists want to see if Komodo dragons could live on other islands. Zoos are also trying to raise Komodo dragons.

Komodo dragons only live on a few islands in Indonesia. They may become **extinct** if a bad storm hits the islands. People must respect Komodo dragons and protect this important lizard.

extinct – no longer living; an extinct animal is one that has died out, with no more of its kind.

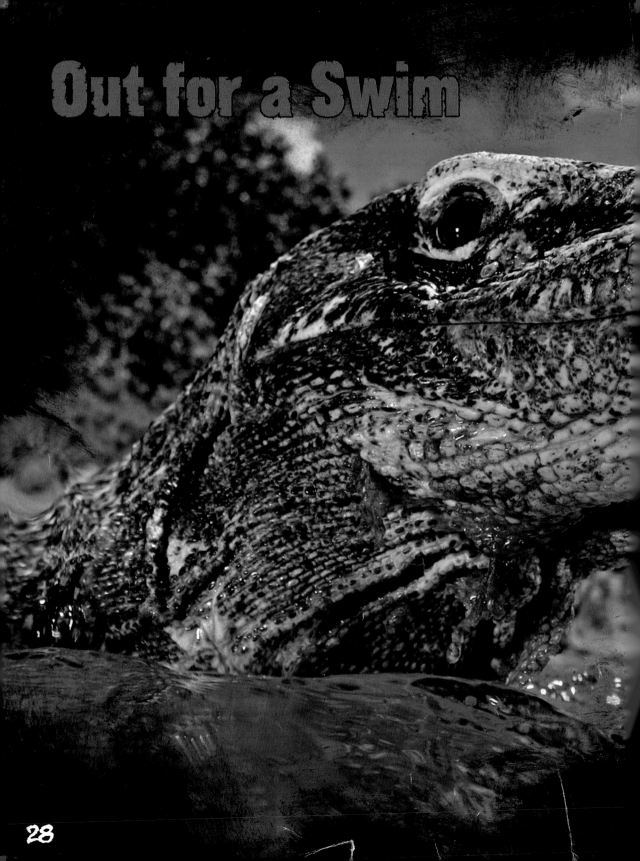

Out for a Swim

Glossary

bacteria (bak-TEER-ee-uh) — very tiny germs

ecosystem (EE-koh-sis-tuhm) — a group of animals and plants that work together with their surroundings

extinct (ik-STINGKT) — no longer living; an extinct animal is one that has died out, with no more of its kind.

island (EYE-luhnd) — a piece of land that is surrounded by water

Jacobson's organ (JAY-kuhb-suhnz OR-guhn) — an organ on the roof of a reptile's mouth

lizard (LIZ-urd) — a reptile with a scaly body, four legs, and a long tail

prey (PRAY) — an animal hunted by another animal for food

reptile (REP-tile) — a scaly-skinned animal that has the same body temperature as its surroundings

Read More

Glaser, Jason. *Komodo Dragons.* World of Reptiles. Mankato, Minn.: Capstone Press, 2006.

Lunis, Natalie. *Komodo Dragon: The World's Biggest Lizard.* SuperSized! New York: Bearport, 2007.

Marsico, Katie. *A Komodo Dragon Hatchling Grows Up.* Scholastic News Nonfiction Readers. New York: Children's Press, 2007.

Internet Sites

FactHound offers a safe, fun way to find educator-approved Internet sites related to this book.

Here's what you do:

1. Visit *www.facthound.com*
2. Choose your grade level.
3. Begin your search.

This book's ID number is 9781429623186.

FactHound will fetch the best sites for you!

INDEX